soccer's new wave

Mia
Hamm

Striking Superstar

By
Rachel Rutledge

THE MILLBROOK PRESS
BROOKFIELD, CONNECTICUT

M

THE MILLBROOK PRESS

Produced by
BITTERSWEET PUBLISHING
John Sammis, President
and
TEAM STEWART, INC.

Series Design and Electronic Page Makeup by
JAFFE ENTERPRISES
Ron Jaffe
Dedicated to Gail Jaffe

Researched by Mariah Morgan and edited by Mark Stewart

All photos courtesy AP/Wide World Photos, Inc. except the following:
Ezra Shaw/Allsport USA — Cover
University of North Carolina — Pages 10, 14, 15, 17, 18, 27
NCAA and Rich Clarkson and Associates, LLC — Pages 19, 28, 29
Daniel Motz/Motzsports — Pages 23, 25
C. Melvin — Page 24
The following images are from the collection of Team Stewart:
Time Inc. — Pages 6 (© 1996), 46 (© 1999)
The Upper Deck Company — Page 26 (© 1994)

Printed in the United States of America

Published by
The Millbrook Press, Inc.
2 Old New Milford Road
Brookfield, Connecticut 06804

www.millbrookpress.com

Library of Congress Cataloging-in-Publication Data

Rutledge, Rachel.
    Mia Hamm: striking superstar / by Rachel Rutledge
    p.   cm.   — (Soccer's new wave)
    Includes index.
    Summary: A biography of one of the members of the 1999 Women's World Cup championship team,
Mia Hamm.
    ISBN 0-7613-1802-X (lib. bdg.)   ISBN 0-7613-1381-8 (pbk.)
    1. Hamm, Mia, 1972– —Juvenile literature. 2. Women soccer players—United States—Biography—
Juvenile literature. [1. Hamm, Mia, 1972– . 2. Soccer players. 3. Women—Biography.] I. Title. II.
Series.
GV942.7.H27R87 2000
796.334′092--dc21
[B]   99-049652

pbk: 1 3 5 7 9 10 8 6 4 2
lib: 1 3 5 7 9 10 8 6 4 2

Contents

Ball of Fire

chapter 1

"Soccer was a way to hang out and make friends."
— MIA HAMM

Teamwork is everything to Mia Hamm. It is what separates her from the other individual stars in women's soccer, and it is what makes her a leader. Learning to be a team player is not easy—the truth is that some of history's most successful athletes never even *tried*. And it certainly does not happen by accident. Often, the process begins early, with unusual kids and a special family.

The Hamm family was definitely a special one. Mia's father, Bill, was a fighter pilot. Her mom, Stephanie, was a ballet dancer. Their six children were bright, athletic, and with one exception, outgoing. That exception was Mia, who was quiet and shy around strangers. At home, however, she was a terror. "I would get attention by screaming and yelling," she remembers.

An emotional child who tended to let things bubble up inside her, Mia needed a way to let off steam. Stephanie Hamm thought that ballet classes would give her daughter the discipline and balance she seemed to need. This experiment, however, was not a success. "I hated it," Mia laughs. "I lasted only one class."

Ultimately, it was Mia's father who provided the outlet she needed. A big sports fan, Bill Hamm had discovered soccer while the family was stationed in Italy, and fell

Could Mia Hamm have found a sport more perfectly suited to her talents and personality than soccer? It certainly was a better choice than ballet!

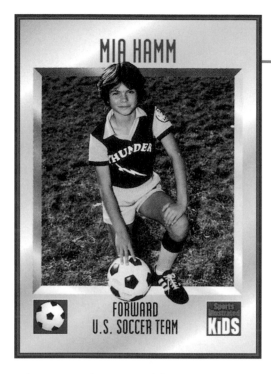

MIA HAMM

FORWARD
U.S. SOCCER TEAM

This trading card, which depicts young Mia at the beginning of her career, has become highly collectible.

in love with the game. Soon all of the Hamms were playing, including Mia, who began when she was just a few years old. It was the perfect sport for her.

Besides being a great way to burn off extra energy, sports helped Mia fit in. Military families must move frequently, which means that their kids must make a whole new set of friends each time they arrive at a new base. Joining a sports team is a way to do this. The Hamms moved from Alabama to California to Italy and then to Virginia—all before Mia reached her fourth birthday. Next stop for the Hamms was Wichita Falls, Texas. This is where Mia began to blossom as a soccer player. She joined her first team at the age of five. "I first played in this pee-wee league," remembers Mia. "Our team record wasn't very good, but I did manage to score a lot of goals."

Although Mia usually was the youngest and smallest girl on the field, she had a good sense of how the game was played. She had watched her older brother and sisters from the sidelines, and had played backyard games with them while their father shouted instructions.

Mia was an instant hit. She could dribble the ball at full speed and swerve around defenders without breaking stride. When opponents ganged up on her, she would wait until the last possi-

Did You Know?

Stephanie Hamm started calling her daughter "Mia" as a baby, because she reminded her of a ballet teacher named Mia, with whom she had once studied. Mia's real first name is Mariel.

ble moment before chipping the ball to an open teammate. Most young players do not master these skills until high school! Mia also began watching games on television. She observed closely how grown-ups played soccer and looked for little tricks that she could practice. The Spanish-language stations in Texas aired lots of soccer matches, and although Mia did not speak Spanish she seemed to understand everything that was happening on the screen.

Mia's biggest booster was her brother Garrett, an Asian-American orphan the Hamms adopted when he was eight years old. Mia, who was five at the time, loved having an "instant brother." The two were inseparable, especially in sports. Their mother called Mia "Garrett's secret weapon," because in neighborhood games no one wanted to pick the shy, quiet little girl. As soon as Garrett was picked, however, he would insist that his team captain choose Mia. In every sport they played—soccer, football, or basketball—they worked together beautifully, whether he was setting her up for goals, tossing her touchdown passes, or getting the ball to her for easy layups. "He shared my love of sports and competition," she says of Garrett, "and nurtured that important part of my life. Also, I think he was the best athlete in the family."

The Hamms lived in Texas for a little over eight years. Part of that time (grades 3–5) was spent in San Antonio, where the level of competition, especially in soccer, was quite high. Most of the time Mia played in boys' leagues, so even though she was an excellent player for her age, there was always someone bigger or faster on the field. Had she limited herself to all-girls competition, Mia would have dominated. But that was not always an option. Besides, Mia thinks that competing against the guys was better for her. "Playing with boys reinforced my will to win and instilled a kind of fearlessness at an early age," she says.

Did You Know?

Mia was the first girl to play Little League baseball in Wichita Falls.

"I'm comfortable expressing myself through soccer. It has everything—fear, frustration, elation. It's the cornerstone of my identity."
MIA HAMM

Texas Tornado

chapter 1

"I see this skinny brunette take off like she had been shot out of a cannon."

— TEAM USA COACH
ANSON DORRANCE

Mia's family moved back to the base in Wichita Falls when she was 12. By this time, she possessed a highly developed set of soccer skills. Mia had the rare ability to go into a tangle of bodies, emerge with the ball, and then explode into a full-speed gallop. Naturally, this caused opponents to tumble into disarray—and that is when Mia was most dangerous.

She was always aware of the entire field, always thinking ahead. With defenders scrambling, she could power her way straight to the goal, or cut across the field while her teammates sprinted into the openings this created. With the whole field in front of her, Mia had all the options—she could launch a strong, accurate shot with either foot, or thread a perfect pass to another player on her team. One of Mia's favorite moves was to pass off, sneak in toward the goal, and then redirect a shot with her head for an easy score.

"I have the best parents in the world. They encouraged me, but never pushed . . . . I had some great role models growing up. So if people want to look to me for inspiration, I take that very seriously. If I can help children realize they can achieve their dreams with hard work and dedication, I'm a happy person."

MIA HAMM

In the mid-1980s, women's soccer was just beginning to develop into an organized, international sport. The game had been played by women for more than a century (especially in Europe), yet few countries funded national teams until the 1980s. In the United States, most of the progress in the women's game was being made on the college level. Programs at schools like the University of North Carolina attracted top-level talent; the women's national team—which was formed in 1985—drew from this pool of players.

Promising young girls like Mia were of great interest to the organizers of women's soccer. Whenever officials heard rumors about a "super player," they listened. What they were hearing about Mia was that she played the game at a different speed than everyone else, and that as soon as she got a little older and a little stronger, she might be the top schoolgirl player in Texas.

By the age of 14, Mia was receiving invitations to a number of regional all-star tournaments. At one of these events she caught the eye of John Cossaboon, who was in charge of the women's national development team. He coached a squad of high-school and college-age kids who would serve as a "pipeline" of talent for Team USA, which had just begun competing internationally. Cossaboon did not expect to find anyone who could

Did You Know?

Mia went out for her junior high school football team—and made it! She played wide receiver and even had a few snaps at quarterback!

make his team—he already had files on all of the best young players. He was in the stands looking for 16- and 17-year-olds he could recommend to some of the nation's top college programs.

Then he spotted Mia. Cossaboon could not take his eyes off of her. In the span of a few minutes, he watched as Mia did everything you could ask of a player. Going almost purely on adrenaline and instinct, she was running rings around everyone else. Why was this young woman not on any list he had seen? Who was she? When Cossaboon was told that she was just 14, he flipped out. Every coach dreams of this moment. He had just seen the future of his sport.

After the game, Cossaboon met with Mia and her parents. He told the Hamms that he wanted her on his development team. Bill and Stephanie asked if Mia was good

enough. Cossaboon told them that, at this moment, their daughter actually was good enough to merit a college scholarship. Mia was totally blown away. She was looking forward to varsity soccer in *high school* that fall. The thought of college and national teams seemed crazy.

To make sure *he* wasn't crazy, Cossaboon talked Anson Dorrance into watching Mia play. Dorrance, the coach at the University of North

UNC coach Anson Dorrance

Carolina and the newly appointed head of Team USA, was naturally skeptical. It was not unusual for a youth-league coach to call or write Dorrance, insisting that he come see the "next great player" in women's soccer. But this recommendation came from Cossaboon, so he decided there might be something to it. Dorrance flew to Louisiana, where Mia was scheduled to play for the North Texas team in a 19-and-under tournament.

Dorrance asked Cossaboon not to point Mia out—if she was as good as advertised, he would know immediately. It took less than a minute to spot her. On a routine play where everyone is supposed to move to a certain place at a certain speed, Mia moved at double-speed, like a character in a video game. Dorrance was riveted. For the rest of the game, he watched Mia effortlessly shed double- and triple-teams, and keep constant pressure on the opposing goal. Dorrance still talks about how Mia "took his breath away" that day.

The Hamm File

MIA'S FAVORITE...

Athletes . . . . Michael Jordan and Jackie Joyner-Kersee. "To have their talent for a day would be awesome."

Individual Sport . . . . Golf. One of her biggest thrills was playing nine holes with Michael Jordan in 1998.

Hobby . . . Playing guitar and singing. "I love music—it's an important part of my life."

Toy . . . . Soccer Barbie, although Mia hates her picture (and goofy smile) on the box. "You can't tell which one is the Barbie!"

Book . . . . *The Prince of Tides*

Food . . . . Pasta

Dorrance knew he had to wait a few years before he could coach Mia in college, but he had no doubt that she could be a contributor to the national team. What worried him was that she would be overwhelmed by the sudden rise in competition. On the international level, the athletes are smarter, faster, and more talented than the best players Mia was used to playing, and in far better physical condition than Mia. Dorrance decided that she could handle the transition, and invited her to try out for the national team that spring.

Stars and Stripes

chapter }

"She came back from that camp wanting two things — to go to North Carolina, and to win the world championship."

— BILL HAMM

Mia arrived at Team USA training camp shortly after her 15th birthday. The first day, the team went into the gym for a few hours of stretching, calisthenics, weight-lifting, and agility drills. Mia had never lifted weights, and never imagined that a soccer player could spend an entire day indoors. When Coach Dorrance called an end to the session, she was glad it was over. She was ready to drop. "When I first did fitness with the national team, I thought I'd die," she admits.

Imagine her surprise when the players sprinted out to the playing field for practice! By the end of the day, Mia was on the verge of tears. She wondered if she would ever be able to live up to this level of training. Everyone else looked so fresh, and everyone else was better than anyone she had ever played against. Yet for all of Mia's misgivings, she sensed that she belonged on this team.

For Mia, the most interesting part of her tryout was seeing how intensely focused the players were on winning. Obviously, this is the point of every soccer game. But Mia had always played for the fun and the challenge and the thrill of making a great play or scoring a spectacular goal. Winning was something that had seemed more important to the boys with whom she played. Mia returned home after her tryout totally excited about soccer. She had seen what the game was like at its highest level. She understood how good she was, but also how much better she could become once she learned about advanced strategies and tactics. Mia also decided that she wanted to play for Coach Dorrance at UNC one day.

Four games into its 1987 schedule, Team USA found itself in need of new players for an August trip to China. Mia could hardly believe it when the phone rang and she was asked to join the squad. She packed her bags and set off on her first international adventure, to the cities of Tianjin and Shenyang. In two games against the Chinese national team, Mia played well enough to earn the respect of her teammates and receive applause from the huge crowds attending the matches. She had never played in front of more than a thousand fans. The roar made by *tens* of thousands of fans caused Mia's hair to stand on end. The excitement was incredible.

Later that year, Mia got permission to take her December break a little early, and joined Team USA for a tournament of Pacific Rim countries. She played against Japan, New Zealand, Canada, Australia, and the host country, Taiwan. Mia learned something new every game, but sometimes she felt lost among so many experienced players. "There were times I played for the national team when I felt like I was always in the wrong place," she claims. "I never knew where to run, why to run, or how to run."

Mia returned to Texas to finish her sophomore year, only to find that the family was readying to pick up and move once again. This time, the Hamms were headed for Burke, Virginia. Although Mia did not relish the thought of having to make new friends again, she immediately saw the bright side of the move: She would be closer to the University of North Carolina, and closer to the other players on the national team, most of whom resided on the East Coast. Also, Burke was located in one of the country's most soccer-crazy regions. The caliber of high-school and club soccer was terrific. The school team she would join in the spring, Lake Braddock Secondary, had reached the state finals two years in a row.

With her life speeding up and her future as a world-class player fairly certain, Mia asked her parents to help her make a plan. She did not see any point in playing high-school ball for two more years when she would soon be one of the best players in the world. Bill and Stephanie Hamm agreed. Mia was good enough to be playing college soccer, and smart enough to be taking college classes. They went to the principal at Lake Braddock and got permission for Mia to double her course load during the 1988–89 year. She would complete her junior year in the fall, and her senior year in the spring. Once the paperwork was done, Coach

Did You Know?

Another young prospect, Kristine Lilly, was also invited to the 1987 Team USA tryout. Mia and Kris became fast friends and, eventually, team leaders. Kris entered the 2000 season with more international appearances than anyone in the history of women's soccer.

Dorrance came calling. He offered Mia a full scholarship to UNC, and she accepted.

Mia met the academic challenge in her final year of high school, and somehow found time to practice and play soccer for the Lake Braddock Bruins. The team's coach, Carolyn Rice, was a bit worried that Mia would not fit in with the team. She feared that her established players would resent someone coming in and being the star of a team that they had worked so long and hard to build. After moving so many times and fitting in so many places, Mia was pretty good at sizing up this type of situation. She decided that she would see where the team needed the most help, and then focus on those areas.

Mia's new teammates were impressed. They could see how hard she was working to become a member of the team, as opposed to being its star. And they saw how embarrassed she was when they asked her what it was like playing for the national team. In no time at all, Mia's modesty and dedication made her both a team leader and a team favorite. The Bruins destroyed their opponents, as Mia joined with Liz Pike and Collette Cunningham to form a front line that struck fear in to the hearts of every goalkeeper in Virginia.

Come playoff time, Mia was unstoppable. In the semifinals, she scored twice in a 5–1 romp over Monacan. In the finals, against Woodbridge, Mia was shadowed by one of the top defensive players in the state, Susan Braun. Braun did an excellent job, but Mia created a couple of fabulous scoring opportunities to give Lake Braddock a 2–1 lead, then scored her second goal of the game to secure a 4–1 win and the state championship. A few weeks after that, Mia was off to the Mediterranean, where she joined Team USA for a match in Sardinia. All in all, it was quite a month!

Tar Heel Terror

chapter 4

"There was no hiding her greatness."

— UNC COACH ANSON DORRANCE

The 1989 North Carolina Tar Heels were the class of women's soccer. The team had won three straight national titles, and had not lost a game since 1985. The Tar Heels also featured Shannon Higgins, the top player in the college game. Mia was inserted into the front line alongside Higgins and fellow Team USA member Kristine Lilly, also a freshman. Coach Dorrance predicted this team would be the most exciting he ever coached, and he was right.

Heading into the Atlantic Coast Conference title game against North Carolina State University, the Tar Heels were unbeaten in 22 games. The real excitement, however, came when the team's normally airtight defense let in three goals against the Wolfpack. Mia and Kris responded to this crisis by blasting two goals apiece to give the Tar Heels a 5–3 win. Mia, already named the ACC's top freshman for 1989, added a tournament MVP trophy to her collection for her fine work that day.

Next stop for UNC was the NCAA Tournament, where the Tar Heels and Wolfpack met again, this time in the semifinals. Once more it was the two "Superfrosh"—Hamm

and Lilly—who scored in a 2–0 victory. It was Mia's 21st goal of the season—tops on the team and the most ever by a college freshman. In the NCAA final, against Colorado, Mia played well again, and Higgins scored the tournament-winner to give UNC its fourth consecutive national championship.

The following summer was a big one for Team USA, which went 6–0 against international competition. Mia was still a sub-stitute, but her scoring prowess (four goals in just five games and 270 minutes of play) made it hard for Coach Dorrance to keep her on the bench. Just keeping Mia out of his *hair* kept Dorrance busy. Every time he turned around, there was Mia—asking questions, discussing strategy, pestering him with hypothetical situations. She rec-ognized that she was nearing the peak of her physical powers, and was anxious for her brain to catch up.

Mia's play during the 1990 college season showed she was making good progress. As usual, the Tar Heels were favored to win it all. But it would not be easy. Higgins and several other key players had graduated, leaving their positions to be filled by freshmen. The inexperience showed, as UNC lost to the University of Connecticut in a

Coach Dorrance did plenty of celebrating during Mia's college career.

September game. Mia was terrific in the contest, scoring both of her team's goals in the 3–2 overtime defeat. As soon as the game was over, however, Mia understood what she *didn't* do. Many of her teammates had become unglued in the overtime period, and she had failed to take charge and "rally the troops." She would not make that mistake again.

In UNC's very next game, Mia took a major step forward as a team leader. Still reeling from the loss to UConn, the Tar Heels played sluggishly against George Mason University. The game was scoreless with regulation time ticking away. With less than a minute to play, Mia forced a defender to make a bad pass and blocked it with her foot. Mia gathered up the loose ball, sped down the left side, and then cut in toward the goal. The keeper pounced out to limit her shooting angle. With the crowd screaming and her teammates cheering, Mia faked the goalie into committing herself one way, then quickly redirected the ball past her. It rolled into the net with just eight seconds remaining!

With Mia now their undisputed leader, the Tar Heels rolled through the rest of the season and won another

Did You Know?

Mia had a secret "second sport" at UNC: basketball. She was a terror in pickup games, and even joined an intramural team.

NCAA title. Best of all, they smashed UConn in the final, 14–4. "We wanted to bury them psychologically in the first fifteen minutes," Mia says of the grudge match. "And that's exactly what we did."

Mia and Kristine Lilly are all smiles during North Carolina's wipeout of UConn during the 1990 NCAA championship game.

Julie Foudy powers her way past a Danish defender.
Julie and Mia became regulars for Team USA during the 1991 season.

Tomorrow, the World

"You have to understand, women's soccer wasn't on anybody's radar back then."
— JULIE FOUDY, TEAM USA STAR

Back when she was a kid in Texas watching soccer on television, Mia had dreamed of playing in the World Cup. At the time, it only existed as a men's tournament. Now that dream became a reality. In 1990, FIFA, the governing body of world soccer, announced that an official women's world championship would be held in China in November of 1991. The date of the tournament meant that Mia had to choose between devoting the fall of 1991 to playing for the Tar Heels or playing for the national team. It was not an easy choice.

In the end, Mia believed that taking a year off would be a good idea. She saw it as her chance to learn to be a great all-around player. Had she stayed in college, the UNC offense would have revolved around her so completely that she barely would have had to play defense. She would not have this luxury on Team USA. At the international level, games are usually won and lost on defensive mistakes, so everyone has to master this part of the game. Mia had to learn quickly, for Coach Dorrance—who also took

the year off from his duties at UNC—moved her from the forward line to right midfielder, where defense would be a major part of her duties.

When the women's world championship started, no one gave the United States much of a chance—Norway and China were the big favorites. But Mia thought they had a great chance. In the weeks prior to the championship, many of the team's stars bounced back from summer injuries and were completely healthy. Also, at the last minute Kristine Lilly had decided to join the squad. She would play across from Mia, as the left midfielder.

Another reason Mia liked Team USA's chances was that she had just about mastered her new position. In fact, she had become so good at turning an opponent's attack around that Dorrance had abandoned his conservative, defense-oriented approach and replaced it with an aggressive, attacking style that was triggered by Mia and Kris. They would take the game to the enemy and rely on sweeper Carla Overbeck and goalkeeper Mary Harvey to tighten up on defense if anyone broke through.

Team USA began its improbable run at the world title with an opening-round victory over Sweden. Next came a shutout against Brazil. Two more shutouts followed against Japan and Taiwan, as Harvey closed off the goal and Michelle Akers terrorized opponents with a pair of multi-goal games.

In the semifinals, against Germany, Mia and Kris—the two youngest players on the team—choked off the high-powered German attack again and again to secure a 5–2 victory for Team USA.

Mia hits the turf against Japan during the 1991 world championships. She was a key contributor for Team USA, which went on to upset Norway in the final.

Now, all that stood between the Americans and the championship was the Norwegian national team, which was considered the best in the world. On paper, however, the task still seemed impossible. There is no way Team USA could win; Norway had recently beaten them twice, making the U.S. look silly in the process. But games like this are played on grass. And funny things can happen when 65,000 screaming fans start pulling for the underdog.

Despite putting constant pressure on Harvey, the Norwegians managed just one goal. Akers netted a beautiful header to even the score. Meanwhile, Mia was everywhere. She could see Norway's plays developing and, time and again, would sprint over to break them up before they got started. Mia and her teammates were sliding, sprawling, and diving all over the field. Finally, with time running out in regulation, Norway's coach

instructed his players to kill the clock; he planned to dispose of the exhausted Americans in overtime.

It was a critical mistake. With the ball deep in her own territory, Norwegian defender Tina Svensson opted to play it safe and pass the ball back to her goalie, Reiden Seth. Another defender stood close by to guard against any mishaps. It was a play the team had flawlessly executed hundreds of times. But they had never done it with Michelle Akers bearing down on them at full steam.

Realizing what Norway was doing, and sensing that her tired teammates probably would not survive an overtime, Akers charged at Svensson, who did not deliver the ball cleanly to Seth. The biggest player in the tournament at 5-10 and 160 pounds, Akers clipped Svensson and sent her flying as she streaked toward the loose ball. Svensson crashed into the other defender, leaving Seth all alone, a good 20 feet out of position, to deal with Akers, who now had the ball. Mia watched as her teammate casually swerved around the helpless keeper and booted the ball into the net.

The desperate Norwegians had no chance after that. The final whistle blew three minutes later and it was official: The United States was the top team in women's soccer. Some of the players ran around screaming and jumping on one another. Others, too exhausted and shocked to celebrate, simply dropped to their knees and wept.

Mia, Team USA's youngest member, gets to hold the championship trophy in the team photo.

Super-Duper Star

chapter 6

"I've seen a new improved version of Mia since the World Cup. Her confidence level is higher. Her consistency is better."

— **UNC** TEAMMATE **APRIL HEINRICHS**

Mia returned to Chapel Hill for the spring semester and got back to being a student. She also got serious about her relationship with a young man named Christiaan Corey. He was on his way to Marine flight school, and the two began toying with the idea of getting married. Mia also rented a house off-campus with some of her Team USA pals. They had a blast. It was a fun time for her.

To Mia's delight, the Tar Heels had done just fine without her. Kristine Lilly had led the squad to another championship before joining the fun in China, and the freshmen whom Mia had led to the 1990 NCAA cham-

Soccer fans could not wait to get their hands on a Kristine Lilly trading card after she led the Tar Heels to four championships in four years.

*UNC and Team USA star
April Heinrichs*

pionship were now experienced, battle-hardened juniors. Mia had grown a lot, too. This became evident as soon as the season started. She was the best scorer, the most daring passer, and the most tenacious defensive forward in the country. And, many insisted, the best soccer player they had ever seen. In 1992, Mia participated in 25 college games; in those games, she scored an incredible 32 goals and set up 33 more. No one had ever had that kind of season before.

In the ACC championship game, UNC and Duke each sported a 22–0 record. Mia led the Tar Heels to a 3–1 win with three spectacular assists. Those who attended the game are still arguing about which of three passes Mia made was the best they've ever seen. A few weeks later, the Tar Heels and Blue Devils met for a return match, this time with the NCAA championship on the line. Mia was magnificent again, netting three goals in a 9–1 blowout. For the seventh straight year, UNC was the national champion. "It was an exciting and special group," says Mia of the '92 Tar Heels. "I'm glad I was a part of it. It was great to play with Kristine Lilly again and with the freshmen who had matured in the year I took off for the championship."

In 1993, it was more of the same. Opponents played Mia even tougher, yet she continued to produce impressive numbers. Once again, she averaged better than a goal per

Mia races past Sherry Worsham of George Mason University during the 1993 NCAA title game. More than 6,000 fans witnessed Mia's final college appearance—at the time the largest U.S. crowd ever to attend a women's soccer match.

game, and once again she killed Duke in the ACC championship. UNC reached the NCAA final, where its opponent was George Mason. The Tar Heels cruised to a 6–0 win, and Mia scored her final goal as a collegian. When she walked off the field, she owned almost every record in women's soccer. A few months later, she was awarded the Broderick Cup as the outstanding female athlete in all of college sports.

If Mia had to choose a highlight from her final season, it probably would be the day she heard that women's soccer was going to be an official sport at the 1996 Summer Olympics in Atlanta. Four NCAA titles, three Player of the Year trophies, and a world championship suddenly seemed like so much hardware compared with the prospect of Olympic gold.

college *stats*

Year	Team	Games	Goals	Assists
1989	North Carolina	23	21	4
1990	North Carolina	22	24	19
1991	Red-Shirted—Did Not Play			
1992	North Carolina	25	32	33
1993	North Carolina	22	26	16
Totals		**92**	**103**	**72**

NCAA National Champion . . . . 1989, '90, '92 & '93
NCAA All-American . . . . 1990, '92 & '93
Hermann Award Winner . . . . 1992 & '93
Missouri Athletic Club Award Winner . . . . 1992 & '93
Broderick Award Winner . . . . 1993 & '94

Mia was definitely psyched. She had always wondered why, as a teenager, she had participated in "Olympic" development programs and sports festivals when women's soccer was not a part of the Olympics. She had always thought of the Olympics as something Mary Lou Retton and Flo-Jo did. It wasn't a "soccer thing."

Now it was a different story. Team USA had a chance to perform on a world stage, in front of untold millions of sports fans. The championship in China was barely reported in the United States, and the largest crowd ever to watch a women's match in the U.S. was probably the 6,000 fans who showed up for Mia's final college game in 1993. If Mia and her teammates could pull off a win at the '96 Olympics, they could put women's soccer on the map.

Mia (left) joins her teammates to show off the 1993 NCAA National championship trophy.

The Face of Women's Soccer

"If Mia walked down the streets of Manhattan, she would have no fear of being mobbed — unless she ran into a bunch of 10-year-old soccer-playing girls!"

— **DAVID HIRSHEY, SPORTS EDITOR**

During the two years leading up to the 1996 Olympics, soccer began to pick up momentum in the United States. In the summer of 1994, the men's World Cup was held in America. The U.S. team did better than expected, and the women's team got some good publicity, too. A set of trading cards (see page 26) was created for the event, and Mia was one of a handful of women players who got her own card. Mia thought it was cool, but also a little embarrassing.

"It's very important for young girls to have female athletes with whom they can identify."
MIA HAMM

Mia's number 9 jersey is the most popular among Team USA fans.

Other opportunities came Mia's way. She began to get offers to endorse products, including Nike cleats. Advertising agencies were conducting research on women's soccer for the first time, and they were coming up with some surprising numbers. Millions of girls played the sport and followed Team USA's progress. They loved to read profiles of their favorite players in magazines like *Sports Illustrated for Kids* and *Soccer Jr.*, and their favorite player was most definitely Mia Hamm. Almost overnight, Mia went from being a complete unknown to becoming a minor celebrity.

Needless to say, they could not have picked a better player for this honor. By the same token, they could not have picked a *worse* one, either. Mia had become a great player because she was such a good *team* player. And a *team* player does not step into the spotlight and take personal bows for her team, much less her entire sport. The whole idea just rubbed Mia the wrong way. "I don't think a lot of athletes walk around thinking they're the best," she says. "If they do, it's probably to hide some weaknesses they have."

The people trying to popularize soccer in the United States—including every member of Team USA—urged Mia to take advantage of this opportunity. They knew it went against her nature, but convinced her how much good it would do for women's soccer to have a "signature player" for future advertisers and sponsors. Reluctantly, she agreed. Like it or not, Mia's face was now the face of women's soccer.

Tony DiCicco replaced Anson Dorrance as Team USA's head coach in 1994.

There was more important news in 1994. Given the mounting interest in the women's game, Coach Dorrance felt he could no longer coach the Tar Heels *and* the national team. He resigned from Team USA, leaving the reins to his able and popular goalkeeper coach, Tony DiCicco. The best news of all came in December, when Mia and Christiaan were married.

By contrast, 1995 was not such a good year. Team USA failed to defend its 1991 championship at the Women's World Cup. Everyone was out to knock the Americans off their perch, and in the semifinals of the tournament, Norway succeeded. Team USA beat China in the consolation game to finish third. A bronze medal was something to be proud of, the players were told, but Mia knew better. After you've won it all, nothing less is acceptable. Certainly, this would be true during the Olympics.

Mia understood that winning anything less than Olympic gold would spell disaster for women's soccer in the United States. "You can be the best soccer ambassadors and not play well

Did You Know?

During World Cup '95, Mia had to play goalie against Denmark when Briana Scurry was ejected. She claims she had no idea what she was doing, but did manage to preserve Team USA's 2-0 shutout. Would she like to play the position again? "No way, I hope I never have to do it again," she says. "I was scared to death. The goal is much bigger when you're inside it than when you're shooting at it!"

on the field, and it's really not going to help the growth of the game," she explains.

It's
Unanimous!

Is Mia Hamm history's best player? Here is what her friends and family have to say.

"She's been a little ball of fire ever since she was teeny."
**STEPHANIE HAMM,
MIA'S MOM**

"Her agility and acceleration set her apart from everyone."
**ANSON DORRANCE,
MIA'S COLLEGE COACH**

"She's the best player in the world."
**TOMMY KAIN,
MIA'S FRIEND**

"Mia is where she is because she deserves it."
**TIFFENY MILBRETT,
MIA'S TEAMMATE**

"Mia understands the game so well, how to make subtle passes and turn average opportunities into great chances."
BRANDI CHASTAIN

Golden Opportunity

chapter 8

"We had a renewed dedication after 1995—we saw our shortcomings and focused on our weaknesses."

— MIA HAMM

From January of 1996 right until the Olympics that summer, the members of Team USA lived, ate, and played together. They talked constantly about what it would take to win the gold medal—what they would have to do as individuals, and what they needed to accomplish as a team. Never had there been a more tight-knit group of athletes focused so completely on one goal. "Everyone committed themselves," remembers Mia, "to being fitter, to being faster, to being stronger and bringing the team closer together, on and off the field."

After winning three games and tying one at a tournament in Brazil, Team USA flew home for two games against Norway. In the first match, Mia scored the go-ahead goal in a 3–2 victory. But in the second contest Norway won on a late goal. The U.S. team had hoped to send a message to the Norwegians: *You can't take us on our home turf.* Instead, it was Norway that sent the message: *See you in July, girls!*

Mia almost didn't make it to July. In a March game against Germany, she collided full-speed with the goalkeeper and lay motionless on the turf as her teammates gasped in horror. Mia was taken off the field on a stretcher. Fortunately, all she had was a sprained knee—it could have been a lot worse. To everyone's relief, Mia recovered quickly.

By the time the Olympics began, Team USA was running like a well-oiled machine. Coach DiCicco had his players ready to meet any challenge. If an opponent decided to take Mia out of the game, the team knew how to make that opponent pay. If an enemy decided to withdraw into a defensive shell, the players knew how to break through. And, most important, if a team scored a fluke goal or two—or if Team USA found itself trailing—there was no chance the players would panic.

Mia battles for position with a Swedish defender during the 1996 Olympics. Sweden's strategy was to keep one player right next to her at all times.

The opening match of the Olympics found Team USA playing Denmark in front of 20,000 fans—a new record for women's soccer in the United States. Despite a blazing sun and 100-degree heat, Mia was sensational, cutting the Danish defense to ribbons with two magnificent scoring plays. Many of the sportswriters and television stations covering the event were seeing Mia for the first time. They were astonished.

In Team USA's next match, the Swedes were waiting for Mia—and they had no intention of letting her beat them. During the game, they assigned one player to cover

Mia did not mind being roughed up during the celebration after Team USA's overtime win over Norway. During the game, the Norwegians had fouled her constantly.

Mia at all times, and whenever she attempted to win a loose ball, they slammed into her. A half-dozen times, Mia was sent crashing to the ground; each time she got up. Finally, the Swedes accomplished their goal. Mia sprained her ankle and could no longer stand. Team USA still won, 2–1.

China was next in the round-robin tournament. With Mia unable to play, the Chinese concentrated on defense and waited for Team USA to make a mistake. Coach DiCicco's players committed no errors, but could not score, either, and the game ended in a 0–0 tie. That was good enough to get the Americans to the semifinals, where they faced their archrivals from Norway.

At game time, Mia was still hurting. Although she was nowhere near 100 percent, she decided to go out there anyway. Mia expected the Norwegians to play a physical game and knew that, if she were on the field, they would target her for extra punishment. This in turn might free up a teammate for a great scoring chance. Mia told the trainer to bury her wounded ankle in tape, and then limped into battle.

The Norwegians pushed, shoved, and kicked her to the ground again and again. On the sidelines, Coach DiCicco was screaming at the referees to call fouls, but his pleas went unanswered. However, as Mia had hoped, her teammates did get all sorts of opportunities to score. But Norway was tough when it counted. Not only did the Norwegians keep the ball out of the net, but they scored a goal to take a 1–0 lead.

Finally, in the second half, officials called a foul on Norway for roughing up Mia in front of the goal. Michelle Akers nailed the resulting penalty kick to tie the match at 1–1. After 90 minutes, the two teams were still tied. But in the overtime, Julie Foudy led "super sub" Shannon MacMillan with a perfect pass, and she scored the winning goal. Although there was still one game to play, Team USA knew it had overcome its greatest challenge. And even though many newspapers reported that Mia had not contributed much to the victory, her teammates knew otherwise: She had played every minute in extreme pain so the team could gain an advantage, and sacrificed her body when another player might have begged to come out.

Four days later, the team met China again to decide who would win the gold medal, and who would settle for the silver. By now, Team USA was one of the big stories of the Olympics. America had fallen in love with the players, and 76,000 people showed up to watch the final. Just a couple of weeks earlier, the players had marveled at the crowd

for their opener. For this game, there were more than three times as many fans—most of whom were chanting, "USA! USA!"

> "We do a lot of appearances and clinics, and we always stay after games and sign autographs. It gives us a personal connection to the fans. The team takes that very seriously."
>
> MIA HAMM

Kristine Lilly threads a pass to a teammate during Team USA's first meeting with China at the '96 Olympics. This match ended in a scoreless tie.

Mia's ankle still hurt, but on the whole she felt much better. She certainly had no intention of being a target in this game. A few minutes into the first half, Kristine Lilly picked up a ball on the left side and worked her way down the field. Mia began sneaking down the right flank. How many times had Mia and Kris worked this play? Lilly made a move to shake a Chinese defender, and at the same time Mia burst into a full run and angled toward the center of the field. Lilly put a pass right on Mia's foot, and in one quick motion she blasted a shot low and hard toward the corner of the net. China's keeper managed to tick the ball with her hand, causing it to ricochet off the post, but MacMillan was right there to drive home the rebound for an easy goal.

The Chinese hung in the game, and scored a beautiful goal to knot the score at 1–1. Meanwhile, Mia's ankle was really beginning to throb, and a pulled muscle was also slowing her down. Afraid she might be hurting the team, Mia offered to sit on the bench in the second half. If her teammates didn't know she was serious, they might have fallen over laughing. Not only did they *want* Mia out there, they expected her to *win* the darn thing!

Mia is not one to shy away from expectations, no matter how high they

Did You Know?

Staying in shape between games is critical to Mia's performance on the field. "I try to work out as much as possible without causing injury from overexertion," she says. "I run, walk, bike, lift weights, do push-ups, sit-ups—normal stuff. I just try to stay consistent."

are. Bolstered by her teammates' confidence, she attacked relentlessly in the second half. Each time she pushed the Chinese into a corner, however, they managed to escape.

Garrett

Mia had little time to savor her Olympic victory, as tragedy struck the Hamm family. Years earlier, her brother Garrett had been diagnosed with aplastic anemia, a rare blood disease. He had had to give up sports, but for a long time he was able to live an otherwise normal life. During the early 1990s, however, Garrett's condition worsened. The treatment for aplastic anemia involves a bone marrow transplant, which is usually donated by a family member. Because Garrett was adopted, a compatible donor could not be found until his situation became very dire.

In February of 1997, Garret got his transplant, and for a time it seemed as if he would recover. But he contracted an infection that his body was too weak to fight. He died that April. "Garrett was, and always will be, my inspiration," says Mia. "Now, no matter where I play, I feel Garrett is there."

It was not until the halfway point of the period that Mia's tenacity paid off. Drawing a group of defenders with a charge down the right side, she noticed that Joy Fawcett had gained a step on her defender. Mia split the Chinese defense with a perfect pass, which Fawcett then redirected to Tiffeny Milbrett, who had found an open space right in front of the goal. Milbrett scored easily to put Team USA ahead 2–1.

A few minutes later, Mia's ankle finally gave out and she had to leave the game. There was no confusion this time about the game she played. Mia was simply spectacular. When the final whistle sounded, she watched as her teammates took a victory lap around the stadium. She hurt too much to join them.

Then they all ran over to Mia and embraced her. It was the proudest moment of her life.

Team USA members jump for joy during the gold medal game following Shannon MacMillan's first-half goal. Mia assisted on the game-winner in the second half before leaving the field with an injury.

Best in the Business

"The way she squares up against a defender—it's like she's saying to her, 'you're mine.'"

— TONY DiCicco

In the years following the 1996 Olympics, Mia Hamm helped to elevate her sport to a previously unimagined level of popularity. Wherever the national team played, tens of thousands of fans came to show their support. Mia was mobbed wherever she traveled, and demand for her autograph went sky-high. Although being famous still embarrassed Mia, she now accepted the fact that being a celebrity brought nothing but good things to the national team.

As for Mia's on-field performance, she just kept rolling along. In 1997, she had a wonderful season, scoring 18 times in 16 games. In 1998, Mia led Team USA to a gold medal at the Goodwill Games, scoring both goals in a 2–0 win over China in the final. Later that fall, she tallied her 100th career goal. As the 1999 season began, Team USA started to focus on that June's

Did You Know?

10% of the price of every 1999 Women's World Cup ticket purchased with a MasterCard was donated to the Mia Hamm Foundation, which supports research for bone marrow diseases and the empowerment of girls in sports.

Women's World Cup. It was being held in the United States, and sell-out crowds were expected at every match. Once again, the eyes of soccer would be on Mia and her teammates, as they sought to pull off an unprecedented "triple"—holding the Olympic, Goodwill Games and World Cup titles simultaneously. As the tournament neared, the pressure mounted.

A number of major corporations had begun to invest sponsorship dollars in women's soc-

Mia watches her shot elude Brazilian goalkeeper Didi. It was her 108th goal, which gave her the career scoring record for women's soccer.

cer, so it was very important for Team USA to win. Also, a lot of people had jumped on the Team USA bandwagon after the Olympics, and did not understand how fierce the competition was. The players suddenly realized that these new fans simply assumed the national team would win all the time. They liked having such confident supporters, but it made them a bit nervous.

Mia was not immune to the pressure. It was *her* face appearing in television commercials, magazine ads, and billboards all over the country; she knew who would get the blame if Team USA came up short. Adding to her problems was the fact that her husband, Christiaan, was departing for a six-month tour of duty in Japan, leaving Mia alone on the second anniversary of Garrett's death. She did manage to score her 108th career goal that spring—making her the top scorer in history—but she also suffered through a frustrating eight-game stretch when she could not buy a goal.

For the first time, people could see the tension in the face of women's soccer.

Cup Crazy

chapter 10

"Our success is as a team, not me as an individual."

— MIA HAMM

Once Women's World Cup '99 started, it took about 17 minutes for Mia to shake out of her funk. With a full house watching Team USA take on Denmark at Giants Stadium in the opening match, Mia took a pass from Brandi Chastain and tried to chip it over defender Katrine Pedersen. The ball hit Pedersen in the chest and bounced right back to Mia, who drilled a booming left-footed shot over goalkeeper Dorthe Larsen. "Are you kidding me—I don't score goals like that," Mia says of her awesome blast. "I leave that to Michelle Akers. That felt good!"

You knew it was a big goal for Mia. Instead of her usual "aw-shucks" smile,

Did You Know?

Mia and her teammates painted their finger nails and toenails red and blue for the Women's World Cup.

she ran around the field with her arms and knees pumping, soaking up the crowd's energy and savoring her goal. "You get so few opportunities," she says of her post-goal victory dance, "that's why everyone celebrates so much when they score."

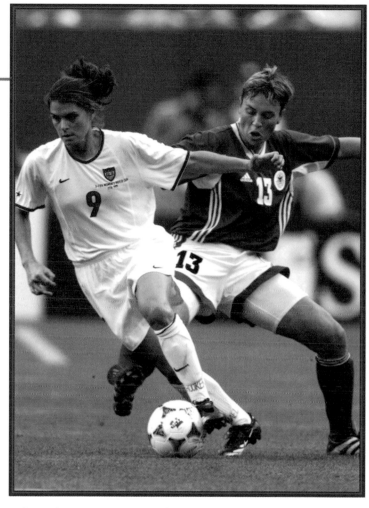

Mia had to take charge against Germany after a defensive mix-up put Team USA behind by a goal.

After disposing of the Danes, 3–0, Team USA trounced Nigeria, 7–1, and beat North Korea, 3–0, to advance to the quarterfinals. Mia and her teammates were a little nervous for their next game against Germany, in part because the President and First Lady were in the stands. Coach DiCicco pleaded with his players to stay focused, and warned them that the Germans were good enough to make them pay for sloppy mistakes.

At halftime, they realized how right he was—Brandi Chastain had mistakenly deflected a ball past keeper Briana Scurry and into her own goal, and Germany scored again right before time ran out to take a 2–1 lead. Team USA really had to turn it on in the second half. Chastain scored a goal to tie the score, then Joy Fawcett came through with a lovely header to make it 3–2. Team USA had just barely averted a catastrophe.

Against Brazil in the semifinals, the defense tightened up and Scurry was sensational at goal. Julie Foudy scored an early goal, and Team USA made it stand up the rest of the way. Mia was marked closely by the Brazilians, and fouled repeatedly. Finally, Brazil was whistled for an infraction against Mia close to the goal, and Akers nailed the penalty shot for a 2–0 victory.

In the final, the Americans met the Chinese, just as they had in the Olympics and Goodwill Games. The two teams knew each other well, and each was quite capable of beating the other. China was the tournament's most technically brilliant team. The Chinese players wasted little motion when they had the ball, and were always thinking two passes ahead. A mistake against this group was likely to result in a goal. The Americans were a little bigger and faster, but the greatest difference was their creativity. DiCicco's women had played together for so long that they could practically read one another's minds. A subtle nod or quick glance was sometimes all that was required to trigger a brilliant play.

More than 90,000 fans—the largest crowd ever to witness a women's sporting event—jammed into the Rose Bowl in Pasadena, California. Forty million more watched the final on television. Tickets were selling for up to $1,000. In short, it was a major happening.

On the field, the two teams probed and sparred and tested each other through regulation time and two overtime periods. China kept a careful eye on Mia, limiting her options at all times. Team USA did the same to Sun Wen, China's most potent offensive player. After more than two hours the score stood at 0–0. The game would be decided by a shootout!

international *stats*

Year	Team	Games	Goals	Assists
1987	USA	7	0	0
1988	USA	8	0	0
1989	USA	1	0	0
1990	USA	5	4	1
1991	USA	28	10	4
1992	USA	2	1	0
1993	USA	16	10	4
1994	USA	9	10	5
1995	USA	21	19	18
1996	USA	23	9	18
1997	USA	16	18	6
1998	USA	21	20	20
1999	USA	26	13	16
Total		**183**	**114**	**90**

World Cup Gold Medalist . . . . 1991 & '99
U.S. Soccer Female Athlete of the Year 1994-1999
Olympic Gold Medalist 1996
Goodwill Games Gold Medalist 1998
Women's Sports Foundation Athlete of the Year 1997
ESPN Outstanding Female Athlete 1998
All-Time Leading Scorer 1999

Each team selected five players to take turns blasting shots from 12 yards away. In a nerve-wracking game of cat and mouse, the goalie had to guess which part of the net a shooter was aiming for, then sprawl in that direction the instant her foot touched the ball. With a little luck, the keeper might get a hand on the ball and make the save. Then it would be up to her teammates to make the rest of their shots count.

China scored on its first two shots, but Carla Overbeck and Joy Fawcett kept Team USA even. China's third shooter, Liu Ying, tried to put the ball into the right corner, but did not kick it far enough toward the post. Scurry, guessing correctly, dove

Mia is congratulated by Sara Whalen (left) and Shannon MacMillan after her kick gave Team USA a 4–3 lead in the shootout against China.

to her left and blocked the ball. Now all the Americans had to do was make their last three shots and the World Cup was theirs.

First up was Kristine Lilly, who calmly scored past goalie Gao Hong. China converted its next kick to make it 3–3. Next, Mia booted the ball in for a 4–3 advantage. Sun Wen

Mia has been on more than a dozen national magazine covers. Her popularity has helped women's soccer become a "mainstream" American sport.

took China's final shot and scored, to make it 4–4. Chastain ended the drama with a clean kick past Gao, then stripped off her jersey and dropped to her knees. Team USA had done it, and this time Mia was right there with her teammates for the wild celebration.

Although she did not score after the tournament's second game, Mia was voted to the World Cup All-Star team. Her contributions, as always, were immense. The fact that she did not "steal the show" only confirmed what she had been maintaining for years: As much as she has grown and as good as she has become, Team USA—and all of women's soccer—has grown and improved even more.

Mia Hamm is still the game's top player, but to her great delight, dozens of new stars have begun to close the gap. And to her immense relief, women's soccer is more than just Mia. "I know what I do out there," she says. "I know where I fit."

Indeed she does. But Mia also knows that there is always room to improve. "Until I can head the ball with the authority of Tisha Venturini, pass with touch and imagination of Kristine Lilly, shoot with the thunder of Michele Akers, and command the team with the grit of Carla Overbeck and the wit of Julie Foudy," she says, "I'll keep striving to become a complete player."

Does Mia ever wish she had avoided the glare of the soccer spotlight and taken a different path? No way! "I have no regrets about the way soccer has played a role in my life," she says. "I am very lucky to have been able to play for my country since I was 15 and have had amazing support from my family, friends, and coaches along the way. I have great friends from the sport and outside of the sport... I love the game."

Mia gets the crowd pumped up before a WNBA game at the Charlotte Coliseum.

Index